Zen Dog

for Gemma

HarperCollins*Publishers*
77–85 Fulham Palace Road,
Hammersmith, London W6 8JB

www.harpercollins.co.uk

First published by HarperCollins*Publishers* 2010
1

A catalogue record of this book
is available from the British Library

ISBN 978 0 00 732069 1

Printed and bound in China by Leo Paper Products Limited

ZEN DOG

There was once a very
IMPORTANT dog.

He had a big office, a sharp suit, a fast car and the very SNAZZIEST of communications devices. And programmed into that communications device were the details of all the most INFLUENTIAL dogs in this big, big city.

One day, on his way to an extremely important meeting, the dog cast half a lobster sandwich into a dustbin. (Didn't you know that dogs LOVE lobster sandwiches?)

"Ow!" said an ant, appearing at the rim of the dustbin. "What are you doing?"

"I might ask the same of you," replied the dog indignantly.

"Well then," said the ant, wiping a dollop of mayonnaise from his forehead, "I shall tell you. I was minding my own business... and playing my TROMBONE."

"That's ridiculous!" laughed the dog. "An ant playing a trombone!"

"Not as RIDICULOUS as a dog in a suit with a lobster sandwich," retorted the ant.

"And besides, in my trombone there is MAGIC. In my trombone... lies the secret... of LIFE." And with that, he picked up a miniature GOLDEN instrument and began to play.

The melody was more haunting and **LYRICAL** than anything the dog had ever heard before. It washed over him like a river of clean, pure **BEAUTY** and penetrated deep into his very soul.

At that moment, the dog caught sight of a single, tiny flower growing between the cracks of the pavement... and he began to **WEEP**.

"What has happened to my life?" he wailed. "Oh, what have I become?

Such simplicity, such humble beauty in this little, PERFECT bloom...

What does a dog need of a suit? Why does a dog need a snazzy communications device?"

And, being careful to avoid the ant and his beautiful instrument, he discarded them both in the dustbin.

"Come, ant," said the dog, "we have a journey to make." And together they set off towards the edge of the city.

"Oh, ant," sighed the dog, "Feel the warmth of the soft, FORGIVING earth beneath your feet. Feel the sun on your back and the wind in your cheeks. What a gift it is simply to be ALIVE on this rich and beautiful planet.

"All my life I have been FRIGHTENED… frightened of losing what I have worked so hard to gain.

But we can't lose the sunshine. We can't lose the flowers. We can't lose the JOY of friendship or the privilege of laughter.

"Oh, how RICH we really are, ant. For the first time in my life I feel truly HAPPY. For the first time in my life... I feel FREE!"

"Indeed," agreed the ant. "Now just imagine if EVERY dog in this big, big city felt the way that you feel right now."

"Yes," said the dog. "Just IMAGINE."

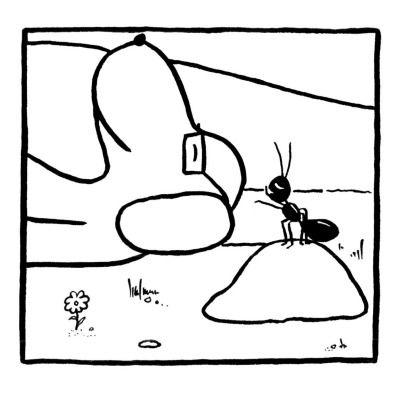

When they arrived home, the dog reached into a dustbin on the pavement.

"What are you doing?" cried the ant. "In that dustbin lies everything that was WRONG with your old life."

"I may be **HAPPY**," said the dog, as he retrieved his communications device, "but I'm not **MAD**"… and he began to type.

And what has happened now, you may ask, to the dog and the ant?

The dog now drifts in a small boat from wave to wave, wherever the breeze decides to take him.

"Happy now", he murmurs to himself, "HAPPY… NOW." And he taps occasionally on a small device in his hands.

And the ant? Well, the other dogs have begun to receive MYSTERIOUS messages...

...Strange exhortations to look outside their windows as, one by one, an ant appears before them.

A tiny ant with a beautiful, GOLDEN trombone.